# BILLY IDOL

## by KATE RUSSELL

JULIAN MESSNER  NEW YORK

TO THE FAMILY MEMBERS IN
MINNEAPOLIS,
FARGO, AND
NEW YORK,
WITH DEEP GRATITUDE.

Copyright © 1985 by Laura Fissinger

Manufactured in the United States of America

Design by Irving Perkins Associates

**Library of Congress Cataloging in Publication Data**

Russell, Kate.
Billy Idol.

Discography: p.
Summary: Traces the career of the young English
musician Billy Idol, who rose to prominence as a member
of a punk rock band and went on to become a superstar.
1. Idol, Billy—Juvenile literature. 2. Rock musicians
—England—Biography—Juvenile literature. [1. Idol,
Billy, 2. Musicians. 3. Rock music] I. Title.
ML420.132R9 1985    784.5'4'00924 [B] [92]    84-25807
ISBN 0-671-55479-4 (lib. bdg.)
ISBN 0-671-55474-3 (pbk.)

# CONTENTS

Billy Idol

# INTRODUCTION

REBEL YELL!

It comes up from audiences all over the world in a tidal wave of noise, motion, raised arms, and love.

Rebel yell!

It comes down from stages all over the world in a tidal wave of sound created by a tall, slender, muscular young man. If a bolt of lightning could look like a human being, it would look like this one.

He has three inches of white-blond hair that seems to glow as it jolts up from his scalp. His eyes are blue-gray and electric with feeling. His mouth is curled up on one side in an expression that's half smile and half snarl. His cheekbones and facial features are handsome enough to qualify him for modeling.

Colored stage lights sparkle off his clothing and jewelry—earrings, shiny neck chains, studded leather belts and bracelets, black leather pants and top decorated with still more jewelry and bits of cloth in bright shades. On the strong arms are little rivers of color where his sweat has begun to run the dye from the leather. His fist is encased in a black leather glove and raised in challenge and greeting. On his left upper arm is an elaborate and beautiful tattoo of a woman named Oktobriana, who's a symbol of fighting for freedom. No one else in rock-and-roll history has ever looked quite like this man does.

Behind him, a four-piece rock band with a hurricane force pushes their classic rock music to the limits of volume and energy. The best part of sixties, seventies, and eighties rock melt together in the heat of their sound. And who's the blond man, singing his heart out, making it all happen?

You already know. Who else could it be?

It's Billy Idol!

Billy's not just dancing with himself anymore, that's for sure. He's one of the biggest stars in today's rock world. He's been called the handsomest man in that world, the poster boy of modern music. One of his LPs has gone platinum, another has gone gold, and a mini-LP has sold over 300,000 copies. Each of his singles has ridden high on the charts. Hundreds of thousands of devoted fans have seen his sold-out concert dates, from New York to Los Angeles and a thousand big and small places in between. His videos are among the most creative and exciting in all of pop music, so innovative that people have called them "three-minute movies."

So what does this good-looking, talented young British man have to rebel against or yell about?

If you listen to Billy's music very closely, you'll hear what he's trying to say. This book will help you to understand Billy's message better, too.

Ever since he was a little boy, Billy has been rebelling and speaking out, in one way or another. He rebels against the pressure in society to conform; he tries to speak out about the importance of being yourself—your real and true self. His music yells encouragement to the fans: the best thing you can do for other people is to be *you*. Keep changing and growing, and don't get scared if other people call you "different" or "weird." You *are* a special person, and you have something unique to give to your family, and your friends, and the future.

"That's my rebel yell," Billy says. "I'm always trying to stick to what I believe in."

Even though he is so handsome, talented, and successful, Billy's not liked by all music critics and fans. Why not? Billy believes it's *because* he is being himself and sticking to what he believes in. Although many people will like you just fine when you're being yourself, he thinks, some people won't, because they get uncomfortable when someone looks or acts differently than they do. But here's the catch—people are almost always somewhat "different" when they're being themselves!

This book is about Billy's struggle to be himself, as a musician *and* as a person. It's about how being true to his personality and beliefs sent Billy to the top of the music world. Sure, Billy likes it best when people like him—but he knows that their approval is only worthwhile if it's in response to his real self. Their love for his music is only valuable if the music comes from Billy's heart.

Billy's fans do love his music, of course. And as you'll see in this book, all of Billy's courage and hard work are paying off. He hears his rebel yell coming back to him from his fans. He hears them say what he'd said himself in "Dancing With Myself": "Don't stop!"

Billy won't stop, that's for sure. Read on, and find out who the handsome blond man is, and why nothing can stop him now.

# CHILDHOOD: BILLY THE KID

WILLIAM BROAD was born to a middle-class English family on November 30, probably in 1956 (Billy won't tell!). His dad, also named William Broad, was a salesman who tried hard to support his family. Billy's mom was an Irish housewife who sometimes worked in the construction industry.

After going through a bad spell in his business dealings, Mr. Broad thought about taking his family to America and trying his luck there. His wife had relatives in the New York City area, so at least they could count on a welcome.

When young Bill was almost four years old, the family settled in the Rockville Centre area of Long Island, New York, not far from New York City. Billy said to reporter

David Keeps: "My earliest memory is being on a boat, going to America when I was about three. I lived in Long Island for the next five years. It was great! You go to school for half a day and watch cartoons when you get up and before you sleep, and you dream all the time. It was just like Disneyland!"

Billy loved New York and he loved America—the excitement, all the different kinds of people, all the hustle and bustle. Not only did he go crazy for cartoons, he also went crazy for rock-and-roll music. Gene Vincent and Elvis Presley were among the American rock stars whom he heard, and they completely captured his attention and imagination. Billy's mind whirled when he heard their big-beat sounds.

But Mr. Broad missed England, so the family went home. By that time, Billy had a crewcut and an American

Since childhood, Billy wanted to belong and fit in, but he also wanted to be himself.

accent. Some of his schoolmates called him "Yank." "People categorize each other a lot more in England," Billy once said. Needless to say, Billy didn't like being teased.

Some kids called Billy worse names than "Yank." Since Mr. Broad kept the family moving around to different towns in southern England because of his work, Billy was often the outsider and the new kid in his school. This became a conflict for him. One one hand, he wanted to belong and fit in. But on the other hand, he wanted to be himself. To accomplish both wasn't easy.

Just as troubles with schoolmates bothered Billy, so did school itself. Billy was a smart youngster, especially at reading. His curiosity about the world in general was very high, and he was anxious to learn. There was a whole big world out there just waiting to be discovered!

Billy didn't like school, though. He felt that kids were talked down to, and weren't given credit for what they already understood. Billy was eager to be taught *how* to think, but he didn't want to be taught *what* to think. So he started to read things on his own.

"I tried to educate myself," Billy explained to *Seventeen* magazine. "That's different from schooling. I read literature. I wanted to know what people thought about things. To know who the people were that were being talked about, and what they said, and why they bothered."

It seemed to Billy that some teachers didn't want to bother with him. They criticized him for wearing his hair "funny," and some of them didn't like the fact that he spoke his mind. He even got expelled from some schools.

A chemistry teacher was particularly irritated that Billy

refused to be interested in his school work. A report was sent to Billy's parents that said: "William is idle."

"My parents were pretty mad about that report," remembers Billy. He was sort of mad about it, too, but it *did* give him an idea for a name that would come in handy later.

If school wasn't satisfying some of Billy's curiosity about the world, though, rock-and-roll music was. "In music, you seemed to get some sort of respect," Billy told *Seventeen*. "The lyrics would try to give you answers . . . or at least reiterate the questions. They didn't tell you to go and be normal just because it was safer to be that way."

At the time Billy started to listen to rock, the pop music world was exploding with new and exciting sounds. Billy just fell in love with the Beatles, and the Rolling Stones, too. "She Loves You" by the Beatles was the very first record he ever bought. The seeds of William Broad's future were planted in the rebellious and hope-filled music of the 1960s rock revolution (called the British Invasion because the music invaded American rock and took it over).

Around the age of ten, Billy was given his first guitar. He learned three chords, and for a long time he just kept experimenting with those three. Sometimes his little sister, six years old, would listen. But when Billy met people who could play better, and they asked what he could play, learning more chords became very important.

Yet Billy knew he already had the most important ingredient of good music inside of him. "In rock, it's not what you do with the instrument, it's the emotion and feeling you put into it," Billy said. "Hearing the music in your mind, that's where it really starts."

"In rock, it's not what you do with the instrument," says Billy, "it's the emotion and feeling you put into it."

As he grew into his teen years, Billy's love for listening and playing rock music increased. In addition to his early heroes like Elvis, the Beatles, and the Rolling Stones, a new batch of super-rowdy American bands caught his attention. Among Billy's new favorites were New York's Velvet Underground, the New York Dolls, Detroit's Iggy Pop and the Stooges, and the MC5, also from Detroit. These bands were actually starting the first punk movement in rock. They were the groups that inspired the English punk revolution in the late seventies that Billy would be a part of.

Obviously, Billy was buying lots of records. What they cost just didn't matter—he had to have them! Later in life, Billy would want everyone to care about rock music with equal intensity. As school became more and more unsatisfying, the urge to go out there and play rock music got stronger and stronger.

Ironically, Mr. Broad's intense dislike for music and musicians made Billy like music even more. "When are you going to get ready for a respectable career?" Mr. Broad asked his son. Unlike Mr. Broad, however, most British people regard pop music as a fairly respectable way to earn a living, especially for kids with little formal education or money.

So Billy moved out of his father's house when he was around the age of sixteen. What great luck, he thought, to find something like music that could be fun *and* meaningful at the same time. The heart of urban London was where most aspiring rockers hung out, so Billy went there.

Even though he was itching to make music of his own, Billy spent the first months on his own watching musicians in clubs. Middle-of-the-road, commercial rock didn't interest him—the blues players and "pub rockers" were the ones that had heart, imagination, and feeling. As far as Billy was concerned, the rock at the top of the charts was made by boring grown-ups who had no idea what kids were about, people who had long ago lost the true spirit of rock music.

Some of Billy's time was spent doing odd jobs to put bread on his table, such as delivering tools to building sites. But the rest of his time was spent with his new friends. Although they didn't know it then, many of these kids would go on to create the punk explosion in England (which turned out to be the second British Invasion in the United States). Some of Billy's friends ended up in influential groups like the Clash and Siouxsie and the Banshees.

After a while, Billy and his friends were nicknamed "the Bromley Contingent," after the section of London in which they hung out. They spent lots of time watching an increasingly famous punk band called the Sex Pistols. They also enjoyed experimenting with their clothes, jewelry, and hair. Billy dyed his hair several colors, before a friend helping him to color it once again caused a fortunate accident. It turned white-blond. But Billy really liked it, and his hair has been that unusual color ever since.

In fact, Billy liked most everything about his new life. It was filled with adventure, creative people, rock music, and fun. Billy kept on watching, listening, and learning. The time was coming soon to start making music of his very own.

# GENERATION X:
# READY STEADY
# GO!

ONE OF the first things Billy did when he was ready to rock was to change his name. He remembered his chemistry teacher's remark; it also made him grin to think of the funny names that certain rock stars of the fifties and sixties had given themselves. One singer Billy remembered had named himself Billy Fury!

William Broad also started to think about the way people declared their so-called stardom in pop music by what they named themselves and their bands. "I can be an idol just by calling myself one. That's how flimsy it all is," Billy laughed to *People* magazine. In *Seventeen,* he explained his choice more completely: "I wanted people to see my sense of humor. Like my name. It can really turn people off, but they should see through it, really. It's simply to poke fun at big stars like Rod Stewart and Mick Jagger—not putting them down, really, just making fun."

Actually, though, the exaggerated sense of self-importance of some established rock stars really bothered Billy a lot. He felt that show-biz attitudes were one of the reasons that music had gotten so bombastic and boring. What had happened to rock's sense of emotional honesty and courage? What had happened to its sense of fun?

When he and bassist Tony James started working in a band called Chelsea in 1976, they were sure their music would be honest and fun. "Our principle idea was that we weren't just musicians,". Billy once said. "We were people who wrote songs about real situations, emotional or factual . . . we didn't care about recording contracts. We *knew* we were going to get the audiences. We were the only thing fresh, young, and exciting of all punk bands. We didn't know it was going to go wild like it did. . . . All this new music around in the eighties is because young punk people pushed for free artistic expression. The existing groups didn't want that. We forced it to happen."

Very shortly after Chelsea started, Tony and Billy left to form their own group, Generation X. Billy remembers the early days of that band as a wonderfully creative time.

How did the creativity of punk music change the sound of rock-and-roll? Well, mostly it made it simpler again. The seventies had been an era of tremendous technical advancements in instruments and studio equipment. When groups went into the studio to make records, they were confronted with an overwhelming number of new choices—all of a sudden, guitars, drums, voices, keyboards, and the rest could make thousands of new sounds they'd never made before. Synthesizers were available that could transform keyboards, instruments, and even the human voice! Stage shows sounded different than ever before.

Consequently, many groups got worried about sounding old-fashioned if they didn't use as many of these new sounds as they or their producers could figure out how to make. Unfortunately, many bands drifted too far away from the raw, spontaneous, and emotional sound that rock had been loved for since its birth in the fifties.

Bands like the Clash, the Sex Pistols, and Generation X used modern sounds and brand-new machines very cau-

Billy and friends with Mick Jones of The Clash.

tiously. Sometimes they'd skip synthesized sounds altogether and just use "old-fashioned" sounds and instruments. Punk *was* sort of old-fashioned in that sense. But it was being made by young people who were eager to rethink the traditional elements of rock music. So it ended up sounding old-fashioned and modern at the same time.

Although Generation X was a punk band, they were different from other punk bands. Their songs were more melodic, and sounded more suited to commercial radio. There was also some great humor in their lyrics, even though those lyrics were often meaningful like those of other punk groups.

What made record companies finally give contracts to these angry and wild-looking young rebels with their daring music? Billy once tried to explain it. "We'd all been complaining about pop music for a long time. Finally it seemed like we should quit complaining and do some music ourselves. There were enough of us in London to do what we wanted. By the time the record companies started giving contracts, it was because we already had built up huge audiences who loved our music. They could make money from signing us because so many kids were ready to buy punk records. Record companies couldn't pretend we didn't exist anymore."

Sure enough, there were plenty of Generation X fans ready to buy records when they finally came out. From 1977 to 1980, the fans danced to great hits like "Your Generation," "Ready Steady Go," and "Wild Youth." There were also three Generation X LPs released during those years—*Generation X, Valley of the Dolls,* and *Kiss Me Deadly.* Most of the music was written by Tony, and most of the words were written by Billy.

Although Billy and Tony had some problems finding

the right musicians, and even changed most of the band members toward the end of the band's life, those difficulties weren't the final blow. What was? It turned out that their manager had been taking money from the band over a rather long period of time, without its knowledge. When Billy finally found out, there was nothing he could do to get the money back. Not only that, but this man fixed it so that the band had to play concerts under a different name for close to two years. The group simply couldn't withstand this financial disaster and emotional stress. Billy left the group.

But he didn't give up on music. Sure, he felt badly. "It could have made me think I didn't want to be in the music business," Billy said, "but I really did want to keep going." And besides, he said, all his troubled times were making him feel more sympathetic toward other people and the hard times they might be going through in their

A 1978 photo of Billy with Mary Travers of Peter, Paul and Mary.

own lives. Especially his fans. These problems made Billy want to write songs about being brave and facing scary situations with all the courage you could manage.

During these hard times, some good things were still happening for Billy. First, he met Keith Forsey, the man who produced the final Generation X LP. (Keith later won an Oscar for co-writing the song "Flashdance.") At the time Billy met him, Keith had been working a great deal as a writer, producer, and player in the European disco scene with important people like writer/producer Giorgio Moroder and singer Donna Summer.

Billy and Keith hit it off. Billy particularly appreciated Keith's ability to make the rhythm in a record really leap out and "hit you in the face." He also respected Keith's talent for working with a broad variety of musical styles while still letting each artist's special personality shine through. Billy wondered if he and Keith just might work together some time in the future.

The second good thing that happened was that the final Generation X single, "Dancing with Myself," had become an underground import hit in American dance/rock clubs. That got Billy thinking about America.

After all, Generation X was finished. He loved London and he loved his friends, but he felt constricted by his reputation as a member of a certain musical movement. A new scene with new people and new possibilities was a very tempting idea. Billy wanted a fresh start and harder musical challenges; maybe then he could make his own music, the way he was beginning to hear it in his head. Mental photographs of his New York childhood flashed through Billy's head. What about New York? he wondered. Would that be the place where it all could come together at last?

# STATESIDE

ONCE BILLY made the decision to move to New York, he felt like it was the right thing to do. He told *Creem* magazine about his situation as he changed cities in 1980:

New York is very like London, very sophisticated, and very gutter as well. Once you've handled a big place like that, it's just minute differences. So I was a lot more worried about whether I was ever going to be able to write a song again. Just like when we started Generation X, there was no money involved, no career, no Billy Idol the lead singer. It was Billy Idol, just being himself, hanging out, starting to move and figure out where he wanted to go.

Moving to a brand-new city can be pretty scary for anyone, even someone as confident as Billy. And it's even scarier when you're moving to try to make it big in your career. Billy believed in himself and in what he'd learned with Generation X, yet he was quite aware that New York was already filled with thousands of young people desperate to make it in the rock business. Hundreds of them had already had some success, like Billy, yet they weren't doing very well. The competition was going to be tough. And even though Billy was sure that London wasn't right for him now, homesickness was definitely going to be a part of those first months in New York City.

Billy also knew that his struggle would be made even more difficult by his unwillingness to compromise. He wasn't going to change his leather clothes or white-blond hair or his outrageous jewelry. Nor was he going to act like anyone but Billy Idol, even if some people didn't like him.

Billy was not willing to change his leathers, his hair or his jewelry, even if some disliked him.

The transition for his career was also going to be complicated by the fact that Billy wasn't really a punk rocker anymore—not completely, anyway. He had made his reputation in punk, but it was time to move away from that, too. "I just felt that music should be more up, more fun, something that makes you feel good instead of depressed. Something that people could dance to," he said in an interview. Pure punk was actually falling out of fashion by 1980, but Billy knew it would take time before people realized that he was a versatile musician and performer.

The first thing he needed to do was find people for his new band. Meeting people to play and write songs with was his top priority. "I thought there would be enough things in my music," Billy said to *Circus* magazine, "that people would be able to overcome any prejudices they had about me."

So Billy started to get used to his new life in New York City. He didn't have much money—sometimes, at first, he slept in Central Park! Eventually, Billy got a place to live in a funky section of lower Manhattan.

Young people trying to make it in creative fields often settle in this part of New York. Many of them are involved in theater, dance, visual arts, or music. Billy found that he liked these people, and soon began to feel more relaxed. He made new friends just doing one of his favorite things—walking city streets at night, watching and talking to people.

Another favorite activity was one he'd enjoyed in London—going to clubs to hear bands. Luckily, it didn't cost too much to get into some of the clubs. Certain places let Billy in for free because he was a former member of

"Billy possessed the true spirit of rock-and-roll."

Generation X. One night, something wonderful happened in a club called Hurrah's. Billy was absentmindedly watching the empty dance floor when suddenly the dance floor filled with people. What was the song that got them on their feet? It was "Dancing with Myself!" Billy watched the dancers with great happiness. Maybe I'll make it here after all, he thought.

Actually, Billy already had someone powerful in his corner, pulling for him. This man's name was Bill Aucoin, and he was a very famous manager in the rock business. Because of him, a heavy-metal band called Kiss had become one of the most successful rock bands the world had ever known. Aucoin was looking for new bands to manage when he had met Billy during the final months of Generation X.

Aucoin had immediately loved Billy's voice, charisma,

and music. "I was looking to retire from the image of that, well, crazed heavy metal," Aucoin laughed to *Performance* magazine. "I knew I had to get away from it when I had Mötley Crüe asking me to manage them! But genre aside, I look for an act that has a certain determination to make it, to see through what needs to be accomplished. Kiss had that determination. Perhaps some of the other acts I worked with couldn't see it through that far. But I could see that Billy had that willingness to push and accomplish those things that truly develop a following for an act." Aucoin also felt that Billy possessed the true spirit of rock-and-roll, something he hadn't seen for a long time. He liked the fact that Billy wanted a lot of control over the management of his career, and that he wanted to do a lot of touring.

Particularly after his experience with the Generation X manager, Billy was wary. Aucoin, however, felt *right*. "Bill was the only manager who never spoke to us about money. He talked to us about why we're doing it, what the reason was. He was willing to work for us for nothing for two years, and spend a lot of time with us," Billy told *Performance*. "We never even had a written contract until everything was together. There was a real element of trust."

Aucoin had urged Billy to move to the United States for the establishment of his solo career. Now that Billy was there, and Aucoin was still rooting for him and trying to help, Billy was reassured.

However, Bill and Billy didn't tell anyone about their relationship at first. They both worried that people would think Billy was just out to be a big pop star, or that he was going to go heavy metal! The two men figured they'd wait

illy Idol with Steve Stevens

until there was something to show people, something that would prove that Billy wasn't a supercommercial pop star or a heavy-metal hero.

Someone else who would end up being very important to Billy came into his life at this time, too. Aucoin introduced Billy to a young, classically trained American guitarist named Steve Stevens. Steve had seen Generation X when they'd played in New York in 1978, and he remembered how much he'd liked Billy's music and stage presence. Steve was quite eager to meet Billy.

At first, these two musicians just hung out together having fun and going to clubs to hear live music. Steve liked Billy. "He was a man of determination—real straightforward. And we wanted the same things out of music." They became very close friends right off, but serious musical work didn't begin until months later. One day, Billy invited Steve over to his house where they played their guitars together for the first time. And from that point, their collaborations on Billy's music would become a source of joy to both of them. (Steve didn't work in a key role on Billy's first solo record, however.) Billy knew he'd found the partner he wanted. They were alike enough that they could agree on many things, yet they were different enough that each brought something unique to the music.

Finally, Billy's musical career looked like it was in good shape. Chrysalis, Billy's record company, was ready to release his very first solo mini-LP. Keith Forsey produced it. What a team, Billy thought—Bill Aucoin, Steve Stevens, and Keith Forsey. How could he lose?

# THE SHOOTING STAR

EVER SINCE struggling with those first three guitar chords at age ten, Billy Idol had been working very hard at his music. But the year 1981 marked the start of a three-year period filled with the hardest work Billy could have imagined. He knew it would be worth it, though. As he told *Knight News* Wire reporter Gary Graff, "If your heart is in the right place, you will get a great audience, and they *will* care."

In preparation for his debut mini-LP, *Don't Stop,* Billy concentrated on clarifying his musical ideas. Coming up with exactly the right kinds of songs, arrangements, and overall moods takes most young musicians a long time, no matter how talented they are. Bill was no exception to that rule.

"If your heart is in the right place," says Billy, "you will get a great audience, and they *will* care."

Some ideas were already clear, though. He knew he wanted the raw energy and fun of pop punk bands like The Ramones. He wanted the heavy rhythms of reggae bands and disco music. He also wanted the lyrical intelligence and the melodic beauty of mainstream rockers like Bruce Springsteen, as well as the modern electronics and artistic daring of synthesizer pioneers like Germany's Kraftwerk and New York's Suicide. What a tall order! Could he combine *all that* into one sound? Could it be a popular sound, too?

As Billy told rock columnist Lisa Robinson: "I am involved in *popular* music. I don't want to make art music or music that's locked away. I want it to be on the radio. I feel like part of the instant culture, and I'm excited by that. But I want to make sure that I'm part of the instant culture that's good."

*Don't Stop* was a good record. Yet when it first came out in 1981, it wasn't very successful. Recorded inexpensively in Los Angeles with session musicians, it contained four songs. The first single was a remake of a sixties American hit called "Mony Mony." It was a fun song and a great dance track. Why didn't the radio stations play it?

Billy has said in interviews that he thinks part of the problem was his image as a wild British punk. American radio programmers felt very nervous about punks in 1981, no matter what country they were from! If radio programmers (the people that pick what songs a station will play) think they'll scare away advertisers by playing a certain kind of music, they won't play it.

Billy saw how radio programmers were reacting to him, but he refused to change. "I didn't change my image when radio didn't play 'Mony Mony' because of my spiky hair," Billy explained. "Some people in rock-and-roll go to heavy metal or synthesizers or whatever the new trend is

Billy's image didn't always sit well with American radio programmers.

that they think is coming. But we've stuck to who we are, and I think that's important."

At the same time that Billy was confronting the radio programmers' resistance to him, something was happening in the music industry that would change it forever. This was the birth of Music Television, MTV, the cable channel that plays music videos twenty-four hours a day. MTV was ready and willing to take chances on new music—after all, they were just starting out, like Billy! Billy Idol and MTV looked like an ideal match simply waiting to happen.

Pretty soon, Billy and his "team" were working on his first full-length LP, simply called *Billy Idol.* There was a super high-energy cut on the album, written by Billy, called "White Wedding." That's the one that was picked to be Billy's first video.

Billy was very excited about this new medium, but he felt cautious, too. "I won't do a video unless I feel confident that it has to do with my ideas and sincerely reflects what I believe," Billy said. "A lot of people don't care, but if I'm going to do something, it's because I believe in it. A lot of groups don't have visual ideas, and they're just forced into doing it. The biggest problem is that a lot of video producers treat groups with the same disrespect they gave to singers like Fabian in the sixties."

Billy picked David Mallet to direct "White Wedding." Mallet, who'd worked with Billy on a 1977 Generation X concert, had directed videos for artists such as David Bowie. Billy liked Mallet's work. As he later said in an interview on MTV:

I wasn't really sure how the "White Wedding" video would turn out. I'd never done something like that.

And it was interesting to find out that . . . well . . . I thought it worked. The fact that I could do something I'd never done before and be happy with it was a revelation to me. I'm not an actor, I'm someone who writes songs and walks about the streets and hangs out with people. Doing something like this was different.

The video was a huge hit on MTV, and it was also a boost for Billy's career. "MTV was one of the few things that allowed me to start a relationship with an audience here," Billy told *Performance* magazine. "When I first got here, and for the first two years, even through the time of 'White Wedding,' the radio would not play my records. . . . MTV put my songs up in front of an audience that was then able to make up its mind about me one way or another. It was just a tremendous stroke of luck because it came along just at the time we had the 'White Wedding' video done."

That's why "White Wedding" didn't appear on *Billboard's* Top Ten until eleven months after its release in late 1982.

The choice for a follow up to "White Wedding" was an unusual one. It was "Dancing with Myself," the Generation X single! Chrysalis Records' West Coast promotion director Steve Brack explained the choice to the *Los Angeles Times*:

Normally we could have just waited until Idol's next album came out, but "White Wedding" was such a big hit with a lot of Top Forty stations which had never played Idol before that we decided to pull out an old song that most people never heard when it came out on *Don't Stop* in 1981. It fit in better with what was being played when it came out the second time.

For this, his second video, Billy chose the famous horror-movie director Tobe Hooper. "It was great working with Tobe," Billy enthused. "He found it a little hard to relate, because he's used to horror movies! But the special effects were really good and he really cared about what he was doing."

People were listening—and watching—at last! Billy hoped they were getting his message. The message in "Dancing," Billy explained, was about "people who look like they have everything under control, but they may not really have it that smooth. The song's about wanting to be involved, wanting to be a part of society, but wanting to do it on your own terms."

Some people, Billy knew, would still not get his message because of the way he looked. More than a few people thought he looked plain goofy! "They can laugh if they think I look stupid," Billy said to *People* magazine. "If they get a laugh out of it, that's kinda cool."

He didn't even mind much if all these new people who were just discovering him didn't like his message either. "You may not like it," Billy said, "but you'll see I mean it." The fact that he meant it, of course, was part of the reason why things were going so well for Billy by mid-1983.

By the summer of 1983, after trying out a few players on *Billy Idol* that didn't end up staying with him, Billy finally had the band he'd always wanted. First, of course, there was Steve (who'd actually *quit* playing in groups

With keyboard player, Judi Dozier.

before joining Billy because he was bored and frustrated). Then there was bassist Steve Webster from Toronto, Canada, who'd been in a great band called Parachute Club. Drummer Tommy Price had played with Mink DeVille as well as Scandal. Last but not least was keyboardist Judi Dozier, a classically trained pianist from North Carolina who'd been trying to make it in New York for a few years when Billy found her.

"Billy gives me a lot of respect both as a woman and as a player," Judi said in *International Musician* and *Recording World*.

At last! Billy knew when people heard this band that they'd know he was doing *real* rock-and-roll, with a *real*

The Billy Idol band

rock-and-roll band. This wasn't a group of hired musicians like the ones he'd worked with on *Don't Stop*. This was an ensemble, a *team*.

"We wanted people who had personalities to contribute, not just noise to make. And you have to get along with each other, or else you can kill the music. We like each other a lot. And we all love the music. We think alike about it. And everyone who works with me knows that *they matter*—and in an age when music has become more manufactured, that's pretty special."

Not only did the band start playing live dates, but they also started to make their first album together as a group, Billy's second album. The dream was coming true—it was almost time for Billy to let loose with a rebel yell. Was the rock world ready to listen?

# THE YELL THAT SHOOK UP SHOOK UP ROCK-AND-ROLL

THE SCENE is a New York City recording studio, in the late summer of 1983. Outside it's so hot that the air feels like an oven. Inside, though, the studio is cool.

The studio is filled with oddly shaped hallways and small rooms, with spare pieces of band equipment scattered about. In one of the rooms there's a coffeemaker and refrigerator, set across from a large and empty couch. Nothing appears to be happening.

But behind a certain series of closed doors, there's something special going on. Billy Idol is listening to those dreams of his coming true.

At the soundboard in the control booth sit producer Keith Forsey and his engineer. Near the walls of the small booth stand a few band members, a journalist, and Billy's publicist. Each one is moving to the thunderbolt of music coming out of the speakers.

Billy Idol is moving harder than anyone. The eerie lights are shining on his movie-star features, making them look even more intense than usual. He has his fist up by his shoulder, like always, softly punching the air to the beat of the title track from his new LP, *Rebel Yell*. His smile is electric with pleasure; this record is the result of a year and a half of hard work, and Billy is pleased with the results.

Then another of the album's cuts, "Blue Highway," comes on. Everyone keeps smiling and moving. The room is flooded with energy. Billy looks like he's going to explode.

Of course, since that hot summer night, Billy's career *has* exploded. Within six weeks of its release, *Rebel Yell* went platinum (that means it sold at least one million copies). The singles from the album, "Rebel Yell," "Eyes without a Face," and "Flesh for Fantasy," all became hits. Billy really was beginning to combine the strengths of sixties, seventies, and eighties rock, and the public was responding. And the sales of *Rebel Yell* sparked the sales power of *Don't Stop* and *Billy Idol*. Eventually, *Don't Stop* sold over 300,000 copies, and *Billy Idol* went gold (sold over half a million copies). At one point, *all three* records were in the Top 200 LPs chart in *Billboard* magazine.

Billy made three videos, one for each of the singles. Once again, their popularity on MTV, as well as network television video shows, helped the record sales. The video for "Rebel Yell" was a first for Billy in that it was

Billy signs autographs after the release of *Rebel Yell*.

simply film of the band playing. Billy wanted to do it that way because he wanted people to see how much the band "cared about the music."

Billy always wants to be one of the bosses on every project he gets involved with, of course. But sometimes he works too hard, like he did during the filming of the video for "Eyes without a Face." He worked for more than thirty hours straight in front of powerful studio lights, special effects, and smoke. His eyes became extremely irritated, and some of their membranes were damaged.

"During that taping there was a lot of heat and flames kicking about, and it really dried my eyes out," Billy told a reporter. "I got tired, so I went to sleep on a lawn outside the studio. A policeman woke me up," he related with some amusement. The officers thought he was a vagrant and were planning to arrest him!

But Billy's eyes were watering very badly, and when he looked up to speak to the officers with tears streaming down his cheeks, the men became alarmed. So instead of taking Billy to jail, they took him to the hospital. Billy was a little shaken by the experience. "It must be terrible being blind. I couldn't remember how my hotel room was laid out. The worst thing was trying to go to the toilet in the night." Billy's injuries were so severe that he had to cancel one concert and postpone a few others. Luckily, his eyes healed up just fine.

A good thing, because there was a whole new world for him to see. For the first time, Billy was embarking on a very long tour. He was itching to go out there and share the experience of live rock-and-roll with all the fans that were giving him so much support and love. "America still likes its music live," says Billy.

"All I want to do now is show people that the MTV version of Billy Idol isn't the same one you'll get live," Billy told the *Hartford Courant*. "There is a lot more to me than that."

"It's been a long, uphill climb for me," he explained further to reporter Barry Millman. "I knew, though, that once I got my band together and my songs together that they'd see the light. *Rebel Yell* is my best record, my most complete record so far. It's *me*, like everything else I've done, except now someone seems to be listening!"

The band was having a great time, too, as they crisscrossed America twice and went to Japan and Australia. "I've always loved high-energy music," Judi exclaimed to *International Musician* and *Recording*

*World,* "and that's why I love playing with Billy. It's a different kind of thrill every night on stage when you're out on the road with him."

It's no wonder that the success of the tour felt like a reward for toughing through all the hard, early days. Billy described the feeling to *Creem* magazine:

> It's great to play in front of 3,000 people. It may not seem like much to some people, but I tell you, it's a lot if you're standing there and getting that reaction. When I feel that, I think it's worth every moment of coming to America.

At last, the press started to like and respect Billy in a big way. Some of the important music journalists had enjoyed Billy and his music since the days of Generation X, but many others had dismissed him as either a rowdy punker or a pretty boy trying to be a big-deal pop star. The reviews for *Rebel Yell* and the following tour were so positive, though, that it seemed like the press was recognizing Billy's talents for the very first time.

Billy's stage presence, charisma, and looks were compared to those of Jim Morrison and Elvis Presley. Some called him the punk movement's first mainstream superstar. It was said that his voice sounded stronger and more interesting than ever before. The reviews praised him for keeping the stage setup and lighting design simple, so that the power of the music and performance were the stars of the show. The writers liked how Billy and Steve danced together, and sparked off each other's high spirits. Many journalists said that the tour was turning Billy's group into one of the best live bands in all of rock.

Billy was finally getting the recognition he had worked toward for so long.

A few writers also praised Billy for touring so much. Many bands in rock cut down on their touring a lot when they start to have platinum albums. Many bands also do fewer live shows if their videos are very popular, because they feel videos are a less expensive, less tiring, and more effective way to reach a large number of people and make new fans. Obviously, Billy doesn't agree.

One question that both fans and writers had during Billy's tour was about the meaning of the phrase *rebel yell*. Although Billy has often said that his songs have many special meanings, this song had only one. As he told one reporter, "Rebel Yell is that feeling you get when you know what you think and believe, and you strive to express it and live it, whether other people approve or not."

Of course, expressing your true self has been Billy's concern from the start. But when he said it one more time, in *Rebel Yell*, people finally heard him.

# CONTROVERSY

BY THE time Billy Idol was a host on MTV's 1984 New Year's Eve Party, it was obvious that he was a major rock star. That's terrific!

But it's also trouble.

It happens all the time in the world of big-time pop music. Artists get very popular and start to have lots of hit records, and people suddenly start finding fault with them. Things that they might have liked when the musician was still struggling, they don't like so much any more. Hairstyles, dress styles, music styles—almost anything a star is or does can be criticized when he or she is thrust into the spotlight of stardom.

Why does this happen? Lots of reasons. One is that

"His hair, his clothes, his sneer . . . people had always found fault with Billy."

when you're popular, the press studies everything about you a lot harder. If they're looking that closely at anything you say or do, they're bound to find something to complain about.

Finding fault with someone can cause controversy, and controversy sells magazines and newspapers. So the press tries hard to find controversial things about a star—and the people who own the publications like the profits from higher sales.

The press and fans also tend to get worried when one of their heroes becomes very successful. They worry that the artist will become vain, or get lazy about their work, or stop caring about the fans that helped make them stars.

Unlike other rock stars, though, Billy had always been controversial. His hair, his clothes, his sneer, his fist in the air, his outspokenness—people had always found fault with Billy. When he became even more controversial after the success of *Rebel Yell*, it seemed like nothing much had changed.

Luckily for Billy, he wasn't very scared of controversy. Sure, he prefers to have people in the press and public like him. He was more afraid, however, of people not feeling *anything* about him, positive or negative. "Love me or hate me," Billy says, "but go to one extreme or another. Don't go down the middle!"

Not that Billy was trying to pump up controversy. "Nothing I do is for an image, really," Billy once said. "Everything I sing or do, I really believe in. It is a bit necessary at times to overexaggerate so that people can understand where you're coming from. But it's all me." In fact, Billy sometimes enjoys it when people react to his exaggerated looks. "People know who I am now," said Billy. "They freak out when they see me dressed like this on the subway. They can't believe it's me!"

As a matter of fact, Billy wears his "Billy Idol look" every time he goes out of his house. "I want people to see that I'm for real," he says, "that I'm me all the time. Sure, it's keeping up the 'image.' But I really do look like this. I'd dress this way even if I wasn't famous. I like it. I don't want to look slick and planned and sanitized. I'm a human being, with good characteristics and bad characteristics. I'm willing to look the fool, as long as I look like *me*."

"For some reason," Billy explained to *Creem* maga-

Billy poses beneath portrait of one of his idols—Elvis Presley.

zine, "because of Bill and the way I look, people imagine that he and I concocted this act. But if we had, by now you'd have had four LP covers *without* spiky hair, not a hint of leather, no big red, black, and white graphics—because the life would have been kicked out of it. For me, what's important is the music—it's what I base the rest of me on."

Certainly Billy doesn't sound like a stuck-up guy, but some people have said that he is. Yet almost every writer that has interviewed him has remarked about how nice he is. They say he seems smart, sensitive, warm, honest, and funny—not at all tough and scary like he sometimes appears in his videos.

After his shows, Billy (who's a vegetarian) enjoys snacks such as chocolate milk, cheeses, fruits, and vegetables. Sometimes he talks to children who find their way backstage. Some loving fans (*especially* girls) can get a little too excited when they get to meet him. After *Rebel Yell*'s success, Billy had to get himself a bodyguard. Veteran bodyguard Ed Parker used to work for one of Billy's heroes—Elvis Presley.

"Elvis was a rebel in his own way," Parker said to *Circus* magazine. "When I realized that about Billy, I quickly grew to love him." Parker even came out of retirement to work for Billy.

Billy may be a big star, but he's still a big fan, too. When the band was in Los Angeles, Parker took Billy to his house and showed him his incredible collection of Presley's belongings. There were capes, belts, rings, and other things. Billy got his picture taken with some of the items. "Hey, I'm just a person like my fans," Billy says. "The only difference is that I make records."

"I'll never lose my integrity," Billy says.

Basically, what keeps Billy cool when people say bad things about him is his belief that it's most important just to be himself—good parts *and* bad parts. Music gave him the confidence and brought him out of himself, and he wants his fans to find that same freedom to be human in *his* music.

"Music is about being closer to people, not farther away," says Billy. "I do music because I care about the music and about people."

Even though he is controversial, Billy believes that most people know he's being himself, and that's more important than whether they like him or not.

"People have come to expect some sort of reliability and honesty in what I say. I've always tried to make music on my own terms," Billy declared to *Scene* magazine. "That's why there are those who try to insult me or cut me down. They know I'll never lose my integrity."

# BLUE HIGHWAY
# TO THE FUTURE

MOST OF the time, when writers ask Billy what he plans for his future, he smiles and says "more music!"

That's probably just what he'll do. He's got the looks, the talent, the songs, the videos, the band, the management, and all the rest of what it takes to keep going in the high-pressure world of big-time rock. Certainly he's got the fans—each of you who has read this book knows that!

But don't think that Billy is satisfied with his music yet. As far as that's concerned, he feels the best of his music is just beginning to happen, especially since the band is so tight from all the touring they've done. Musically and personally they're becoming very close. Billy says that his next album, which he'll start recording in December

Steve and Billy believe that the best lies ahead for them.

1984, will be even more pure rock than *Rebel Yell*—even more direct, powerful, and full of energy. Steve and Billy are very excited about the songs they're writing now, and both believe that the best of those songs are still to come.

Would Billy like to take his message to people through acting? Especially since the huge success of the "White Wedding" video, there has been talk in the entertainment world about Billy going into acting. It seems natural, doesn't it, with his charisma and looks? Billy talked about acting during an interview for *Music Connection* magazine. There was a rumor that he was going to get a part in Tobe Hooper's movie, "Space Vampires."

"I backed out, because music is more important to me. We're in the middle of this big tour, and we have an album to think about. I don't want to be an actor. I'm not really sure of my abilities, anyway. Music is always first, but I wouldn't mind doing a small part. I'd love to be in the next 'Star Trek' movie!"

In his spare time, besides going for walks, listening to

Billy takes time out to cuddle with girlfriend, choreographer Perri Lister.

records, and reading books, he *loves* to watch "Star Trek." Sometimes he asks people at his concerts if they watch "Star Trek," too—they cheer wildly in agreement!

Does Billy have girlfriends? Will he get married someday? Billy, as you surely know, *loves* women, and he enjoys dating a number of girls. But he feels that his life right now is just too demanding to take on a wife and children. Occasionally, he's joked about rocking out for a few more years, then marrying someone rich and retiring forever to a life of leisure! We doubt that he'll do that soon. His music is too important, and Billy's having too much fun right now, anyway.

Speaking of fun, sometimes he and the band get some

pretty crazy ideas about fun things to do. For a while they were talking about masquerading as a heavy-metal band and doing a tour with Twisted Sister.

Mostly, though, Billy Idol just wants to do a great job of making rock-and-roll music for his fans. When Billy talks about his fans, a true tenderness passes through those big blue-gray eyes. The curl of his lip goes away. Everything in his fierce expression softens.

And suddenly, it's not so hard to picture Billy Idol as William Broad, the child, with a head full of ideas and a heart full of caring for people. You can picture his intense concentration struggling with those first chords on his first guitar. William Broad decided the best thing he could do for the world was to be his true self—and he stuck with it!

This is how he described the message in his song "Blue Highway" to *What's New* magazine:

> When you're traveling on a bus like we do when we're on tour, or if you're going on any sort of journey in America, there's always this massive blue sky in front of you. It makes you feel like you can soar into the stratosphere. It made me want to write a song saying that *we had a future,* that it can be right now. At the end of the song I say, "Now there's a time for love." Nobody seems to talk about that much.

Billy Idol is talking about love. He is talking about how loving yourself and being who you are is the best thing you can possibly strive to do. He's saying that loving music can help you find who you are. And to Billy, his millions of fans say: "We love you, too, Billy! Don't stop!"

e sings about love, and that's all you need.

# DISCOGRAPHY

**GENERATION X: SINGLES (released in England)**
"Your Generation"
"Wild Youth"
"Ready Steady Go"
"Dancing with Myself"

**ALBUMS**
Generation X (1978, English release; 1983, American re-release)
Valley of the Dolls (1979, English release; 1983, American re-release)
Kiss Me Deadly (1981, English release, under the name "Gen X")

**SOLO SINGLES**
"Mony Mony" (1981)
"White Wedding" (backed with "Dead On Arrival"; 1982)
"Dancing with Myself" (backed with "Love Calling"; 1983)
"Rebel Yell" (backed with "Crank Call"; 1984)
"Eyes without a Face" (backed with "Blue Highway"; 1984)
"Flesh for Fantasy" (backed with "The Dead Next Door"; 1984)

**SOLO LPS**
Don't Stop (mini-LP; 1981)
Billy Idol (1982)
Rebel Yell (1983)

# ABOUT THE AUTHOR

Kate Russell is a journalist living in the New York area. She loves rock-and-roll (obviously) and thinks that writing about it is almost as good as playing it. She hopes to be the biographer who all the rock stars want to talk to. Someday.

She also likes cats.